Autumn's Eulogy

Eddie Brophy

BookLeaf Publishing

India | USA | UK

Presentation by *BookLeaf Publishing*

Web: www.bookleafpub.com

E-mail: info@bookleafpub.com

ISBN: 9789357445757

First edition 2022

For Dylan and Ryder

The Blood of a Wallflower

With the milquetoast anxiety
coursing through my veins,
I bear witness to the gentrification
of a past wrest from a cultural disease.

The nostalgic panhandlers
of a wholesale zeitgeist
repossess my childhood
but try to sell me back my pain.

You can peel the glow in the dark solar system
from the ceiling,
but I remember being kissed
                              under a dozen neon stars
        dreaming of synchronicity
after suffering several failed kismets.

I hold onto teenage wistfulness
the way a conspiracy theorist
votes for their savior of the week.

A church of bombastic indignation
cultivating towns to abandon children
at the first sign of vulnerability.

The Blood of a Wallflower
is an intangible badge of perseverance when—

—Love is a concept and
    Wisdom is a bumper sticker and
        Pain is the only currency in a world that
prides itself on
        Misery.

Tears of a Saturnine Heart

I was raised to be
so complacent in misery
that I don't even know
how to decipher
the cries of a broken heart
from the diligent compliance
to emotional abuse.

I am chain-smoking my feelings,
homesick for a fictitious meal
—emaciated and alone—
with all the macabre inside
—desperate for a respite—
from the persistent cancer
of sorrow's tapeworms,
imbibing what little is left while
looking for shelter in happier memories.

I'm at the tender mercies
of her indifference,
grieving quietly to myself,
mitigating portions of ennui
through incremental death when
one day I'll just walk away
and she can pretend

that she never wanted me to leave.

Forever Their Moon

Take me to your oceans
even though I never learned to swim.
Let your current carry me away
from the plateaus of loneliness.

No more haunted sandcastles
crumbling under the weight
of a childhood without beaches.
If I drown in you, I'll be emancipated
from the lonely saline lost in
morose bedrooms locked up in myself.

I wish I could've been your seahorse
disencumbered you from my womb
plethoric with melancholy.
I hope you never sequester yourself
from the defensive disposition of your mood.
I understand, that's why I'll be the third eye
hiding behind the cynicism of your youth
if you promise to be my sea.

I'll always be as vigilant
without a measure of distance
because when my sons go down tonight
I'm forever their moon.

Black Mood Ring

She wrote my obituary
on the back of a cocktail napkin
that she fashioned into a rose
like she's poised for my demise
contemplating religion
with the gusto of a truant
while the arbitrary wisdom
of a lemonade stand clairvoyant
seems to have monopolized her mind
she doesn't care that much for serendipity
unless the color of the valentine
matches her most flattering funeral dress
and after I'm buried
by the cumbersome weight
of carrying this futile love
to its final solitude
she'll disinter what remains
of her soul's sordid wrath
the black ring that matched
the last days of my love's maudlin mood

Saudade

Your faustian bribe
can't persuade me
to trade these saudade feelings
and give up on my traumatic youth
if it perpetuates the envy of
genocidal compromise
to cultivate the apathy of your God
and imbibe all the spite
and liquors of Richards
with blasphemous reverence
to the lunacies of inebriated patriarchs
writing bibles to endorse
raping their wives and daughters
I might be contrite
but I'm not lost
in the Apopemptic verses
like a crooked apostle
selling a time share milieu
satori is watching innocent burn
in the counterfeit churches
built by fraudulent prophecies
when the life that never wanted you
becomes the death that loves you
I'm most alive
ostracized from your congregation

False Profit

Demoralized in the sacristy
by a righteous paradigm
only to be repudiated
by their impunity
still the gormless congregate
to heed the toplofty manifestoes
preaching mores, they must adhere
victimhood is subjective
in the eyes of an absent sentient
and clutched in the iron fist of every narcissist
the shallow antipathies of your way
left me bitter toward the velleities
of their obtuse orisons for identity
the vulgarization of your faith
became the mausoleums of your trust
and the myopia of your sanctities
bore the invention of glorified criminality
masticated by the lies
until the eventuality that all prey
will lose their flavor
then it is time to find new real estate
through a revisionist's prophecy
from the churches to the television
from the tents to the white house
the subterfuge of charlatans

still turns a false profit

Perpetual Trepidation

Your milieu of crucifixion does not make me
contrite
it just goads my abstinence of trust
and when self-perseveration fails me
addiction is the lonely bed
I am sleeping my life through at night
quaff the alcohol with the exuberance
of a first kiss, and drown in the ennui
that reality is convoluting the sanctities
and turning my Saturday Morning Cartoons
into the propaganda of political pundits
and other nefarious talking heads
trying to sell me nostalgia for what does not
exist
I want to go to sleep and wake up in someone
else's grave
and give the charity of faith
to the death certificate on my screen
liver failure and an ex-wife
my empathy for the deceased
and their chemical subordination
never meant to become a caustic tryst
but the lust for decadence
monopolizes the sorrows of time
all those tedious hours

sitting at a desk and staring at the clock
is this the place I am going to die?
not even settling for mediocrity
I have acquiesced my potential just to exist

Rationality vs. Religion and Love is Science Fiction

I've never been subordinate

to the idolatry of a saint

but I've experienced unrequited love

and the infidelity of a pathological liar

so, I get religion to the extent

that I've been a pious loser

and been cheated on

by a god who created

a latchkey soul

and sequestered him

with the impunity of

a myopic kind of love

a masochistic heart

like a doomsday clock

a Pavlov dog,

when midnight

salivates

touch me before I become

evanescent

an insecure romance

that kills me

before I realize

life was achievable

but I settled for

her abusive kiss

The Wounds of Their Faults

Another clandestine tryst
and I'm espoused to this cicatrice
knowing that you covet mine
now burrowed in my mind
is a sordid act of hate
and the culpable remain
without empathy or shame
now the wounds of their faults
fester into an unyielding contagion
because the hubris of the narcissist
believes their heart to be infallible
with the impunity of a self-anointed saint
a recidivous sinner pardons their plague
after exploiting the malleability
of the harpy's next carnal conquest
now I forsake the cowardice
of this glorified snake
and the unheeded cries to purge
all the poison from my veins
while they repudiate the wanton hurt
of the ecstasies they've expunged
I'd be remiss to forget
that it will always be this way

A Pious Mistake

They lionize the thief
who expropriated their minds,
enjoying a toothsome buffet of
intellectual real estate
like a cannibal fletcherizing flesh
while basking in the ecstasy of their hate
to deliver another jeremiad of lies
the shibboleth of the masochist
sings a reverence
to resonate with the despot's self-acclaim
while the parasite of their disease
sustains the perils of a vile normalcy
can we emancipate humanity
from its servile solitude?
when the malleable victimhood
becomes a transmutation of volatile shame
it was just a pious mistake
to fall in love with a familiar hurt
and deify its ostentatious pride
until the existential macabre
of unmitigated melancholy
can go back to sleep
but they'll hear the dissonance in their head
until it's drowned out
with white noise until they turn red

The Social Erasure of an Over the Counterculture

A talented junkie
with a penchant for woe
became a wealthy raconteur
through poignant hyperbole
busking for empathy on the radio
until the viability of a jaded zeitgeist
turned him into perilous commodity
then there was a maudlin teen
who was the priestess of her coven
until a patriarchy of megalomaniacs
subdued her soul
and made transcendence futile
before she died with her head
in an easy bake oven
now the evasive vindication
of a bastardized zeitgeist
where the incendiary desperation
becomes an arbitrary trend
sees the world through lobotomy eyes
of the pharmacy boys and girls
imbibing narcotics for Zen
to be the next martyr to lead
they're the over the counterculture

Somnambulist

Placating to the tyranny
of all your lies,
just to cultivate a life
that no longer looks like mine
has left me with tourniquets
around my heart
to stop the hemorrhaging
of assimilating in a reality
I decry
now I'm ambivalent and
bastardized
the least you could do
is emancipate a modicum of truth?
even then, I wouldn't believe you
so, play martyr for your sympathy parade
while you demoralize my faith
I don't need to live
but I don't want to die
I can exist somewhere in between
the cadavers and the sycophants
aren't you complacent enough?
haven't you masticated enough of my soul?
I did not want to be so jaded
I used to believe, and I used to exist
if you had it your way,

I'd be the somnambulist

Crestfallen

My heart feels like collateral
when you're ruminating
over the ambivalence
of how you spend your time
but the tedium is always mine
because your myopic decadence
isn't without consequence
and my somber outbursts
are not without credence
you sent me to my room to color
while you navigate the home
you've always reminded me
doesn't belong to me or my messy childhood
but like a furnishing you can't live without
I'll always be there to pacify
the tension in the room
because I love you forever more
even when you're subduing
the tears I can't withhold
I'll be there to break your fall
hiding anecdotes under your pillow
ransacking your telephone for every reason I
should go
I don't know how to be afraid
and you don't know how to be alone

I wonder if you hear my voice
when you're wistful for someone else's breath

In a Lobby with G.I. Faux

Anesthetized under artificial moons
where rapture is a fleeting mood
and love needs to be disincentivized
from how good it looks
juxtaposed to how it feels inside
when loneliness is proselytizing fate
making kismet a trivial and vapid prerequisite
to the eventuality of a dismal planet
colonized by avoidable cancers
killing organic livelihoods
like a frail nervous system
and the vanity of ignoring a rotten tooth
subordinate to the fashion of identity
until we succumb to the detriment
of being lulled into complacent immolation
for an intangible sense of community
seldom do the enlightened prophesize
that the emancipation from our soul's disease
is by embracing the existential plague
to expunge an entire civilization
as a justification for the volatility
that came out of the melancholic solitude
now the tedium of our lives
are tattooed with the grievances of their lies
if the cult of fear, is germinating faster

with a collateral of graves what will it take to
survive?

Besotted with Woe

You wrote your best fiction
with your lips
and with mine
you let me confide
all the vulnerability
of a lonely heart
but now that you've had
your rendezvous
with your quasi
Marlboro man
I feel so used
by pernicious fate
and an obstinate delusion
I fell victim to her
avarice dreams
that a pauper
could never provide
now the faces from our past
treat me like a stranger
that they never knew
besotted with woe
my head is a refuge
for a sadness
that just won't let go

McEmpathy

A redacted history
of indigenous slaves
narcotized by an education
inundated with falsehoods
from doctored texts
only to strive for
college debt
while making minimum wage
now everyone is dying politely
without making a sound
and the calloused souls
are undaunted by the disparities
of economies endemic of
a detrimental cultural deceit
identity politics
and the heresy of being kind
while a backlog of karmic IOUs
bankrupt the sensitivity
from the rationally defeated
while the disingenuous
franchise humanity
with McEmpathy
would you like more lies with that?

Latibule

It's quiet
when liberosis
sets in
the dolt
of your affection
has me
sojourning in
my latibule
again
like an abused child
stuck in the crawlspace
with a bankie
that smells like
his mother's cigarettes
the humiliation
of another fight
that wasn't over me
proves that
redamancy
is futility
left alone
in this solitude
hoping someone
will love me
enough

and let me out

Method Actor

I tried so hard to repair
all the torment of what
getting that girl back
was putting us through
and when I reached out my hand
you turned away
and walked out on a future
I don't believe
you wanted anyway
so, you can keep
all the tainted memories
they're all just
expendable when
they no longer
excite you like
decadent lust
now you can have
the spotlight you craved
the stage is yours
but the auditorium
is empty.

Meliorism

Voyeuristic fodder
for the social capitalist
masticating drama
with conviction
they don't want
to miss a scene
I found myself
devoured
by a ravenous mob
indifferent
and nihilistic
to the feeling
of seeing you
give your kisses
away
until the angels
and saints
reached out their hands
and begged me
to make it through the night
I am alive
because good still exists
even when
I can't find it
in the one I loved

Autumn's Eulogy

Catatonia is the last refuge
for the broken hearted
and tedious pain
of love's crucifixion
bears the labors
of a philosophic destitution
when faith is executed in the street
while the disingenuous
proselytize their charlatan ways
romanticized by the gallows of sinners
in a cacophony of an apoplectic crowd
my face is bludgeoned
and my soul is demoralized
while you indulge yourselves
in the toothsome voyeurism
of another man's pain
eulogized by the daughter
buried by the sons
autumn's clemency
cauterizes the wounds
while the debt of humanity
collects its bounty
from every vein
I used to be a romantic
until you usurped the integrity

making these frailties insane

Tacenda

Love is not
a labyrinth
and I am not
a rat
sequestered
inside
the puzzle
of you
I am not
an arbitrary piece
you've struggled with
and put away
until you can figure out
where I go
you took away your hand
and for a while
I was a frightened child
searching for a parent
now I'm emancipated
left with unspoken thoughts
our resolution is gone
as it turns out
it was me
I was looking for
all along